Linking Wilderness Research and Management

Volume 3 – Recreation Fees in Wilderness and Other Public Lands:

An Annotated Reading List

Series Editor

Vita Wright
Research Application Program Director
Aldo Leopold Wilderness Research Institute
Rocky Mountain Research Station
U.S. Department of Agriculture, Forest Service
Missoula, MT 59807

Author

Annette Puttkammer
Research Associate
University of Montana Foundation
University of Montana
Missoula, MT 59812
(formerly with the Aldo Leopold
Wilderness Research Institute)

USDA Forest Service
General Technical Report RMRS-79-vol. 3.

September 2001

Preface

Federal land management agencies have recognized the importance of incorporating the best available scientific knowledge into management decisions. However, both managers and researchers have struggled to identify effective processes for accomplishing this objective. The Aldo Leopold Wilderness Research Institute's Research Application Program works toward understanding barriers to the use of science in management and developing ways to make relevant scientific information more accessible. Managers can base their decisions on the best available scientific knowledge only if they are aware of current and relevant science as well as how it fits into their management goals.

The *Linking Wilderness Research and Management* series of annotated reading lists was developed to help land managers and others access scientific information relevant to protecting and restoring wilderness and similarly managed lands, as well as the myriad of values associated with such lands. References in these reading lists have been categorized to draw attention to the relevance of each publication, and then organized to provide a logical framework for addressing the issue. Each volume begins with references necessary to understand the overall issue, and then provides references useful for identifying management goals, understanding influences on those goals, and finally, for selecting and implementing management approaches. For example, the Recreation Fees volume begins with sections on recreation fee history, pros and cons of recreation fees, and fee policy issues. Then it addresses pricing, visitor willingness to pay, and attitudes toward recreation fees, and finishes with sections on the influence of fees on visitation/use and estimating and spending fee revenue. Within each section, articles have been annotated to clarify their relevance to that section and to highlight their importance for wilderness management.

These reading lists were designed to serve a wide audience. First, each list introduces generalists to the breadth of factors that should be considered when addressing a management issue. These volumes also enable specialists to maintain familiarity with research relevant to their discipline but outside their area of expertise. For instance, the Invasive Plants volume may be useful to a botanist who specializes in protecting rare species but is not familiar with the invasive plant literature. For those generally familiar with the concepts, this series facilitates access to literature that can add depth to their conceptual knowledge. Rather than produce comprehensive bibliographies, which may be unwieldy for those with limited time, the authors included overviews, the most current examples of literature addressing pertinent concepts, and frequently cited classic publications. These lists can provide a starting point for readers interested in more detail on specific subjects to conduct their own literature reviews.

To facilitate access to these lists and enable us to update them, the lists are also available through the Aldo Leopold Wilderness Research Institute's Web site (http://www.wilderness.net/leopold). The Leopold Institute is a Federal interagency research institute that focuses on ecological and social science research needed to sustain wilderness ecosystems and wilderness values. I hope this series will help sustain wilderness, similarly managed lands, and associated values by enabling managers, policymakers, educators, user groups, and others to access the best available science on the topics covered.

–Vita Wright, Series Editor

Acknowledgments

We wish to thank Ron McCarville, Tom More, Steve Reiling, and Alan Watson for reviews and helpful comments on the manuscript. We appreciate Alison Perkins', Dave Ausband's, and Amy Cilimburg's help with proofreading and editing. Alison Perkins annotated the references dated 2000 and 2001, and Amy Cilimburg contributed the web site annotations. This work is based on the more comprehensive work by Annette Puttkammer and Daniel W. McCollum, "An Annotated Bibliography Related to Recreation Fees on Public Land." We thank the interagency Aldo Leopold Wilderness Research Institute, the USDA Forest Service, Rocky Mountain Research Station, Identification and Valuation of Wildland Resource Benefits Unit, and the interagency Arthur Carhart National Wilderness Training Center for sponsoring this project.

Contents

I

II

III

IV

V

VI

VII

VIII

IX

INTRODUCTION

The passage of the Recreation Fee Demonstration Program legislation in 1996 marked the beginning of recreation fee programs targeted for users of Federally designated wilderness in the United States. This legislation has different implications for wilderness management than for other recreation programs because wilderness as a recreation resource has unique management policies and directives that may affect whether and how to implement recreation user fees. Wilderness managers implementing fee programs are faced with a variety of decisions including whether to use fees, how to collect fees, set prices, spend revenue, and respond to potential negative visitor reactions to new fees, and how wilderness experiences may change as a result of fees. Research shows there have been both positive and negative responses to recreation fees. This reading list includes references relevant to planning for and monitoring the effects of wilderness fee programs.

SCOPE

To develop this reading list, I selected references from a comprehensive bibliography of recreation fee literature (McCollum and Puttkammer 1999). While the comprehensive bibliography includes all literature related to recreation fees, this annotated reading list includes only papers that address recreation fees on public lands and highlights those articles that are relevant to managing wilderness.

ORGANIZATION

The references are organized by subject to make it easier for readers to access articles that address specific management questions. The reading list begins with an overview of the history of recreation user fees. Next, I've included articles that address the pros and cons of recreation fees, particularly for wilderness, and followed these with papers on fee policy, issues, and research needs. The next section on pricing includes articles on establishing a price, pricing policy and fee program development, visitor response to price and price changes, and determining or altering visitor/consumer price expectations. This is followed by a section on willingness to pay (WTP) and recreation fees; this section addresses WTP as a tool to develop fee programs and explores the meaning of WTP levels. The reading list concludes with sections on attitudes toward recreation fees and how recreation fees influence visitation and use. Each section begins with a brief paragraph summarizing the major topics covered by articles listed in that section.

A list of Recreation Fee Demonstration Program web sites has also been included to help the reader access additional information and resources regarding recreation use fees.

REFERENCE

McCollum, Daniel W.; Puttkammer, Annette. 1999. A bibliography related to recreation fees on public land, [online]. Available (http://www.fs.fed.us/rm/value/research-recfee_bibliog.html). [2001, June 25].

ANNOTATED READING LIST

I. HISTORY OF RECREATION FEES

Recreation user fees have historically been a contentious issue, with public, political, and administrative support shifting back and forth over time. The papers in this section examine Federal agency fee program development, the numerous amendments made to the Land and Water Conservation Fund Act, and other trends and events that contribute to the history of recreation user fees in the 20th century.

Driver, B. L.; Bossi, James E.; Cordell, H. Ken. 1985. Trends in user fees at Federal outdoor recreation areas. In: Wood, James D., Jr., ed. 1985 Proceedings national outdoor recreation trends symposium II Vol. 1; 1985 February 24–27; Myrtle Beach, SC. Atlanta, GA: U.S. Department of the Interior, National Park Service, Science Publications Office: 222–241.

Annotation: This paper considers four trends related to user fees at Federal recreation areas: (1) trends in rationale for fees; (2) trends in Federal agency attempts to obtain broader fee-levying authorities; (3) trends in user fees under existing Federal authorities; and (4) possible trends under broader authorities. The paper suggests that user fees have increased in several agencies (camping fees have increased at a slightly higher rate than inflation). Agencies want to levy a wider array of fees, but are constrained by existing fee-levying authorities.

Mackintosh, Barry. 1983. Visitor fees in the National Park system: a legislative and administrative history. Washington, DC: U.S. Department of the Interior, National Park Service, History Division. 118 p. Can be viewed at: http://www.cr.nps.gov/history/online_books/mackintosh3/

Annotation: This study's purpose is to prepare a comprehensive history of National Park visitor fees. Its purpose is not to arrive at or recommend specific solutions but rather to provide a broader context within which program managers can address concerns.

White, Chris. 1992. Legislative history of outdoor recreation fees. In: U.S. Army Corps of Engineers, Waterways Experiment Station, Recnotes, natural resources research program. Vol. R-92-3. Vicksburg, MS: U.S. Army Corps of Engineers, Waterways Experiment Station: 1–5.

Annotation: Looking back on the history of fee development helps us understand today's feelings about user fees for outdoor recreation. This article describes the long, winding, and complicated legislative path that led to the fee structure present in the early 1990s.

II. OVERVIEW: PROS AND CONS OF RECREATION FEES

Many supporting and opposing arguments for recreation fees are present throughout the literature. Some authors argue that actual users of sites should bear the costs associated with their recreation, that fees increase the quality and quantity of services, and that fees can generate revenues that help agencies cover the costs of services. Other authors argue that it is neither ethical nor fair to base access to public lands on the ability to pay fees, that public recreation is a public good that should be subsidized by the government, and that once introduced, fee amounts will continue to increase.

Anderson, Kristin H. 2000. The debate surrounding newly implemented recreation user fees on Federal lands: an examination of those actively opposed. Missoula: The University of Montana. 120 p. Thesis.

Annotation: See section III, page 9.

Binkley, Clark S.; Mendelsohn, Robert O. 1987. Recreation user fees: II. An economic analysis. Journal of Forestry. 85(5): 31–35.

Annotation: The economic basis for recreation fees involves both willingness to pay and the costs of supplying recreation. These concepts together with a discussion of how fees can allocate use, how to distribute costs and benefits, and how to generate revenue, are the basis of this author's economic argument for increasing recreation user fees.

Cockrell, David; Wellman, J. Douglas. 1985. Democracy and leisure: reflections on pay-as-you-go outdoor recreation. Journal of Park and Recreation Administration. 3(4): 1–10.

Annotation: The authors present a philosophical discussion about outdoor recreation as a public good and the appropriateness of fees. The discussion centers on the ideas of Frederick Law Olmsted, and historical and modern leisure theories. They conclude that outdoor recreation is a public good that should be subsidized, and user fees, when applied judiciously and as part of a well-formed management philosophy, are justifiable. Four general policy guidelines that could lead to management guidelines for user fee systems are proposed.

Crandall, Derrick A.; Driver, B. L. 1984. Recreation on public lands: should the user pay? American Forests. 90(3): 10–11, 49–53.

Annotation: In its investigation of the fee issue, *American Forests* found that most knowledgeable observers seem to believe recreation user fees are inevitable. This article presents two views on fees. Derrick A. Crandall, President of the American Recreation Coalition, puts forth the rationale in favor of a system of user fees, while Dr. B. L. Driver, a Research Forester with the USDA Forest Service, addresses the difficulties that must be faced in implementing such a system.

Ellerbrock, Mike. 1982. Some straight talk on user fees. Parks and Recreation. January: 59–62.

Annotation: This straightforward look at the pros and cons of implementing user fees includes discussions on moral values, egalitarian concerns, and democratic ideals.

Harris, Charles C.; Driver, B. L. 1987. Recreation user fees: I. Pros and cons. Journal of Forestry. May: 25–29.

Annotation: After discussing the evolution of user fees in Federal agencies from the early 1900s to the 1980s, the authors give their arguments either in opposition of, or in support for, recreation fees. Opposing arguments include historic precedent (tradition), public recreation opportunities as a merit good, and the necessity of public subsidies for some segments of society. Supporting arguments include increased quality of recreation services, reduced congestion and resource damage, and that onsite users should bear a larger part of the costs associated with recreation. In conclusion, the authors suggest that fees, although an undesirable necessity, could serve to legitimize recreation management and conserve our wildlands.

McCarville, Ronald E. 1995. Pricing for public leisure services: an ethical dilemma? Journal of Applied Recreation Research. 20(2): 95–108.

Annotation: See section IV.B. page 12.

Miller, Shane. 1998. A walk in the park: fee or free? The George Wright Forum. 15(1): 55–62.

Annotation: Supporting and opposing arguments of recreation fees are discussed. According to fee proponents, the primary advantage of recreation user fees is that they are the fairest source of revenue. They also improve the efficiency and responsiveness of the agency by introducing a context of market economy. Fees can also alleviate problems with overcrowding, and increase public appreciation of the parks. Fee opponents argue that fees are improper because preservation and conservation benefit all of society, and fees are impractical to administer fairly. There is also the possibility that fees will become widespread and increase to levels that are unacceptable but difficult to reverse. Fees are also inappropriate because they limit access on the basis of income.

More, Thomas A. 1999. A functionalist approach to user fees. Journal of Leisure Research. 31(3): 227–244.

Annotation: See section III. page 10.

Reiling, Stephen D.; Anderson, Mark W. 1985. Equity and efficiency in public provision of forest-based recreation opportunities. Journal of Environmental Management. 20: 149–161.

Annotation: See section IV.B. page 12.

Schultz, John H.; McAvoy, Leo H.; Dustin, Daniel L. 1988. What are we in business for? Parks and Recreation. January: 52–55.

Annotation: The authors argue that applying private sector marketing principles to the problems faced by public parks and recreation is not the most appropriate solution. Important public benefits flow from park and recreation services that should not be commodified.

III. Fee Policy Issues and Research Needs

These papers express several perceived concerns about user fees, including the lack of clear agency objectives for fee programs, a shift in agency focus away from the original intent and public purposes of public lands, and the need to consider research in making fee policy decisions. Watson and Herath (1999) caution that economic paradigms on public fee and pricing questions fail to address existing social issues such as displacement, equity, and government subsidies for public goods.

Anderson, Kristin H. 2000. The debate surrounding newly implemented recreation user fees on Federal lands: an examination of those actively opposed. Missoula, MT: The University of Montana. 120 p. Thesis.

Annotation: This study examines the debate surrounding recreation user fees that have been implemented as a result of the Recreational Fee Demonstration Program (RFDP) that was authorized by Congress in 1996. From the perspective of those actively opposed to fees, this study sought to answer the following questions: What are the fundamental reasons for opposition to recreation user fees? What is the context of the opposition, and how is the opposition being framed? How is this opposition being expressed, and what are the objectives of the actions taken? Indepth interviews were conducted with 29 active fee opposers. They based their opposition on ideology, the political process, and program administration. The author notes that the context of this opposition is somewhat based on trust and confidence in the agency administering the fees and the activity for which the fee is charged. The study also produced information about how active opposers express their opposition to fee implementation. Ultimately, the purpose of their actions is to prevent the RFDP from becoming permanent fee policy, or at the least, to influence a revision of the legislation. To do this, publicity is being generated to create an awareness of the RFDP and to make the opposition to it known. Study results are presented in two dimensions. The first presents a conceptual framework describing the fundamental reasons for opposition to recreation user fees. The second is a description of the primary actions taken in opposition to recreation user fees and their objectives.

Cockrell, David; Wellman, J. Douglas. 1985. Democracy and leisure: reflections on pay-as-you-go outdoor recreation. Journal of Park and Recreation Administration. 3(4): 1–10.

Annotation: See section II. page 7.

Goodale, Tom. 2001. Keynote address: Discipline and chaos. In: Proceedings of the 2000 Northeastern Recreation Research Symposium; 2000 April 2–4; The Sagamore on Lake George in Bolton Landing, New York. Gen. Tech. Rep. NE-276. Newton Square, PA: U.S. Department of Agriculture, Forest Service, Northeastern Research Station: 3–7.

Annotation: This opinion paper decries the charge that agencies are to "demonstrate the feasibility of user generated cost recovery." Goodale contends the government has already engineered gross inequities in the tax burden, and that demonstrating the willingness of users to be taxed compromises science and the public perception of the role of science. Moreover, he argues that to demonstrate feasibility of user-generated cost recovery, agencies ascertain and then reshape public perceptions, and in so doing, form and rationalize policy. In his view, policy should be based on information and understanding developed through science.

Martin, Steven R. 1999. A policy implementation analysis of the Recreation Fee Demonstration Program: convergence of public sentiment, agency programs, and policy principles? Journal of Park and Recreation Administration. 17(3): 15–34.

Annotation: This paper examines the relationships among: (1) a set of principles to guide the design and implementation of recreation fee programs; (2) agency fee programs, objectives, and actions; and (3) public sentiment toward recreation fees. The premise of this paper is that Federal agency fee programs (under the Recreation Fee Demonstration Program) would benefit from a convergence of these three factors—that is, that fee programs will be more accepted by the public, and be programmatically stronger, if they use a set of guiding principles as well as reflect public sentiment. Reports on implementation of the Recreation Fee Demonstration Program were collected from the participating agencies. Agency fee program objectives were identified in order to assess the extent to which they put the guiding principles into operation, and to determine if they addressed public concerns, which were obtained from numerous sources including publications, articles, and visitor survey data. Agencies appear to adequately address only four of the relevant 12 concerns identified. With the exception of four principles, the agencies have done an adequate job of putting the guiding principles into operation. One recommendation is for agencies to develop specific objectives for their fee programs that clearly reflect broader agency policy and philosophy. In addition, agencies need to more clearly articulate their criteria for determining when to charge fees.

More, Thomas A. 1999. A functionalist approach to user fees. Journal of Leisure Research. 31(3): 227–244.

Annotation: This paper reviews three major arguments in favor of fees within the context of historical, political, and socioeconomic trends, particularly the rise of libertarianism and the decline of the middle class. The three arguments discussed are that fees: (1) promote equity (fairness in the distribution of costs and benefits) by charging users directly; (2) increase economic efficiency; and (3) generate needed revenue. However, the argument about equity fails to consider the effect of fees on people at the margin, particularly the working class. The efficiency argument relies on questionable assumptions about value and willingness to pay and weights public policy toward the preferences of the affluent. The argument about revenue generation tends to advance agency interests that may be perceived as inconsistent with the interests of the general public. In the debates over the mechanics of setting fees, we have lost sight of public purpose. As an alternative, a functionalist perspective that focuses on the purposes associated with public-sector management of parks and recreation is proposed. Public parks, facilities, and programs must serve public objectives. It is these objectives that determine the appropriateness of user fees.

Watson, Alan E.; Herath, Gamini. 1999. Research implications of the theme issues "Recreation Fees and Pricing Issues in the Public Sector" (Journal of Park and Recreation Administration) and "Societal Response to Recreation Fees on Public Lands" (Journal of Leisure Research). Journal of Leisure Research. 31(3): 325–334.

Annotation: This is the overview paper for the 1999 *Journal of Leisure Research* theme issue on fees on public lands (articles from the 1999 *Journal of Park and Recreation Administration* theme issue on fees are also included in the discussion). The authors summarized their response to the papers in these two journals into a set of high priority research and application questions meant to stimulate thought regarding the future of fees and pricing approaches in the public sector. Issues addressed include: (1) the controversial tradeoffs between considering fees from a public perspective versus a consumer point of view; (2) how fees change the relationship between public lands and the American people; (3) public support for fees and how revenues should be used; (4) who will be affected most by fees; and (5) the importance of research in assessing effects of fees and policy formation.

IV. PRICING METHODS, ISSUES, AND CONCERNS

A. Establishing a Price

Several authors suggest that pricing policies should consider potential influences on visitation as well as the desire to raise revenue. For example, incorporating visitor expectations and ability to pay into price-setting decisions helps to address concerns regarding access to recreation sites. Establishing an appropriate price decreases the likelihood of negative visitor reaction to fees and protects against potential decreases in visitation. This can result in improved revenue potential.

Crompton, John L. 1982. Psychological dimensions of pricing leisure services. Recreation Research Review. 9(3): 12–20.

Annotation: The method for establishing a specific price should consider the psychological impact that price would have on potential clients. The reactions of client groups to price changes are sometimes based on emotion rather than on the rationale and logic of the economist. This paper explores eight psychological dimensions of pricing leisure services and gives some examples of public reactions. The dimensions are: (1) expected price threshold; (2) tolerance zone; (3) client adjustment period; (4) price quality relationships; (5) anchor pricing; (6) changing the perceived value of services; (7) customary pricing; and (8) odd pricing. A routine evaluation of all prices should be undertaken annually, and prices should be adjusted appropriately to reflect changes in objectives, costs, or demand.

Crompton, John L. 1984. How to establish a price for park and recreation services. Trends. 21(4): 12–21.

Annotation: The approach to establishing a price discussed in this article consists of three stages. Stage 1 requires an agency to determine the proportion of costs incurred in delivering a service that the price should recover. Stage 2 recognizes that a service's price must be perceived as reasonable by potential client groups or they will refuse to pay or will vigorously protest through the political process. In stage 3 the appropriateness of varying this price for some user groups or in specified contexts is considered. This approach is an alternative to arbitrarily choosing an initial price with the main purpose being to raise revenue.

Howard, Dennis R.; Selin, Steven W. 1987. A method for establishing consumer price tolerance levels for public recreation services. Journal of Park and Recreation Administration. 5(3): 48–59.

Annotation: This research explores the extent to which public recreation consumers are willing to pay fee increases before expressing measurable resistance. Three kinds of prices (low, medium, and high) were determined for a set of different recreation activities. The low price alternative would recover as much as 50 percent of the costs of producing the activity. The medium price represented the "break-even" point where the fee would cover all the costs. The high price represented the "going rate," or what was being charged for comparable services elsewhere in the region. Pricing questionnaires were sent to 720 randomly selected participants, with one-third of the respondents receiving low price figures, one-third medium price, and one-third high price. Clear price threshold levels were found, and they varied substantially from one activity to another. For example, tennis respondents expressed the greatest price tolerance for increased charges for tennis lessons. In contrast, whitewater rafters responded largely negatively to proposed price increases.

Richer, Jerrell Ross; Christensen, Neal A. 1999. Appropriate fees for wilderness day use: pricing decisions for recreation on public land. Journal of Leisure Research. 31(3): 269–280.

Annotation: An appropriate fee for the use of public lands is one that strikes a balance between the need for fee revenues, the desire to maintain access and four related concerns—fairness, equity, other users' ability to pay, and congestion. Including these concerns in pricing decisions improves the likelihood that fees will be acceptable to users. Data are used from a 1997 to 1998 survey of 407 day-use visitors to the Desolation Wilderness. This paper examines whether the fee levels visitors claim they are willing to pay (at maximum) are consistent with the amounts they feel are appropriate. A demand curve from willingness to pay data is constructed, and then the tradeoff between revenue and access based on the appropriate price criterion is evaluated. A total of 62 percent of Desolation Wilderness day users stated a willingness to pay greater than the appropriate price. The cost of choosing a fee at the median appropriate price ($2), rather than the revenue maximizing price ($5), is a 30 percent reduction in revenue, while the gain is a smaller drop in participation (17 percent versus 52 percent).

B. Pricing Policy and Fee Program Development

Although there are concerns regarding appropriate pricing, some researchers conclude that it is possible to develop a fair fee policy for the delivery of leisure services. They suggest that pricing is often underutilized as a tool to move toward greater efficiency, fairness, and environmentally sustainable management. Additional views presented in these papers include: (1) fees should be raised to make them more efficient; (2) fee increases may not result in complete cost recovery; and (3) pricing decisions should be related to costs associated with providing recreation services, such as operating costs.

Crompton, John L. 1982. Psychological dimensions of pricing leisure services. Recreation Research Review. 9(3): 12–20.

Annotation: See section IV.A. page 11.

Laarman, Jan G.; Gregersen, Hans M. 1996. Pricing policy in nature-based tourism. Tourism Management. 17(4): 247–54.

Annotation: Pricing and revenue allocation in nature-based tourism (NBT) are seriously neglected in public policy, especially for the many governments around the world struggling with fiscal problems. This paper has three objectives: (1) to review the economist's concept of willingness to pay as a basis for NBT pricing; (2) to examine administrative criteria in NBT pricing from the perspective of a government agency; and (3) to discuss the elements of success in NBT pricing at policy and project levels. The issues of multiple pricing objectives, visitor categories, visitor activities, fee instruments, and philosophical positions are examined in relation to improving pricing practices. Some suggestions to improve pricing practices are made.

Martin, Steven R. 2000. Donations as an alternative to wilderness user fees—the case of the Desolation Wilderness. In: Cole, David N.; McCool, Stephen F.; Borrie, William T.; O'Loughlin, Jennifer, comps. Wilderness science in a time of change conference—Volume 4: wilderness visitors, experiences, and visitor management; 1999 May 23–27; Missoula, MT. Proceedings RMRS-P-15-VOL-4. Ogden, UT: U.S. Department of Agriculture, Forest Service, Rocky Mountain Research Station: 142–147.

Annotation: After reviewing previously expressed concerns about charging public recreation fees, the author suggests that donations might be an adequate substitute for fees designed to generate revenue, promote equity, and nurture public support. He notes that studies have found that backcountry visitors prefer donations to mandatory fees. In 1997, fees were established for use of the Desolation Wilderness in California; however, four trailheads and several information stations requested only voluntary donations. Day-use visitors in the Desolation were surveyed to determine their opinions about both mandatory fees and donations. Paying a wilderness day-use fee was acceptable to 49 percent of the respondents. Similarly, 55 percent of visitors using trailheads requesting donations reported making a donation. Evidence from trailheads requiring fees indicated a similar proportion of visitors would donate a similar amount if a donation was requested instead of a mandatory fee. Income was significantly associated with propensity to donate but not with the amount donated. Donations were related to a feeling of similar goals between visitors and the Forest Service and the number of years since the visitor's first day trip to the wilderness. Martin finds that newer visitors comply with donation requests more often but donate smaller amounts than long-time visitors, and long-time visitors have a lower compliance rate but donate larger amounts than newer visitors. Therefore, to increase donation amounts, solicitations should address feelings of place attachment, but to increase compliance, solicitations may focus on continuing need and goal sharing. Other techniques include legitimizing small contributions and promising matching funds.

McCarville, Ronald E. 1995. Pricing for public leisure services: an ethical dilemma? Journal of Applied Recreation Research. 20(2): 95–108.

Annotation: This paper reviews the conceptual and pragmatic issues surrounding the application of public-sector fees. The paper suggests that not all public initiatives are equally deserving of tax support. Consequently, fees are sometimes justified. Further, fees are not inconsistent with the service ethic of the public sector. A pricing policy that uses a strategic approach to pricing decisions is described. The suggestions are designed to reduce the potentially exclusionary nature of fees and charges. The author concludes that fees are dangerous not in their application, but in their misapplication.

Reiling, Stephen D.; Anderson, Mark W. 1985. Equity and efficiency in public provision of forest-based recreation opportunities. Journal of Environmental Management. 20: 149–161.

Annotation: The first objective of this paper is to present the costs of provision data collected for forest-based public outdoor recreational facilities in Maine, and compare them to the fees paid by the users of the facilities. The second objective is to describe the consequences of underpricing these services. The third objective is to analyze some of the arguments that have been used to rationalize the subsidization of public recreation facilities. The results reconfirm what other cost of provision studies have found: user fees at forest recreation facilities fail to cover the costs of providing services. The author concludes that not only does such underpricing lead to economic inefficiency, but it may also represent an inequitable redistribution of society's resources.

Richer, Jerrell Ross; Christensen, Neal A. 1999. Appropriate fees for wilderness day use: pricing decisions for recreation on public land. Journal of Leisure Research. 31(3): 269–280.

Annotation: See section IV.A. page 11.

Rosenthal, Donald H.; Loomis, John B.; Peterson, George L. 1984. Pricing for efficiency and revenue in public recreation areas. Journal of Leisure Research. 16(3): 195–208.

Annotation: This article supports the view that rationing outdoor recreation use by using marginal cost pricing is best because it maximizes net economic benefits. The necessary conditions for pricing outdoor recreation to be economically appropriate are that the marginal costs (arising from overcrowding, ecological damage, and operating expenses) of using the area be greater than zero, and the costs of charging fees not be excessive. Assessing fees for wilderness, dispersed, and lake and reservoir recreation is discussed. In addition to raising revenues, pricing can be a valuable tool to redistribute recreation use over time and space, to encourage people to adjust their timing and location choices to save money, and to help make recreation programs more self-supporting.

Stevens, T.; More, T.; Allen, P. G. 1989. Pricing policies for public day-use outdoor recreation facilities. Journal of Environmental Management. 28: 43–52.

Annotation: Visitors at four State-operated day-use outdoor recreation areas in western Massachusetts were surveyed during summer 1984. A total of 324 completed questionnaires were returned. The questionnaire asked visitors about their visitation, trip and party characteristics, and how the cost of recreation facilities should be financed. Willingness to pay was measured using the statement, "If the law required all costs to be paid from entry fees, and if fees were charged per person, what is the maximum amount you would pay to visit per day?" The willingness-to-pay data were used to estimate site demand, park benefits, and visitor response to different pricing strategies. Annual benefit and cost calculations for the four parks determined that under the current fee structure, only 25 percent of cost was recovered through entry fees. Total benefits were estimated to exceed costs. None of the alternative pricing policies discussed guarantee that a fee increase would result in complete cost recovery. Visitors most frequently chose to finance facilities with an equal mix of taxes and increased admission fees (42 percent). About one-fifth (23 percent) had no opinion, 19 percent wanted an increase in State taxes to pay for the entire cost, and 16 percent wanted an increase in admission fees to pay the entire cost.

Walsh, Richard G. 1986. Pricing practices and market structure. In: Walsh, Richard G., ed. Recreation economic decisions: comparing benefits and costs. State College, PA: Venture Publishing: 463–553.

Annotation: The six main topics discussed in this chapter are: (1) the problems associated with charging users for part of the cost of park and recreation programs and the protection of natural, historic, and cultural resources; (2) evaluating pricing patterns in terms of agency policy, costs, benefits, comparable prices, and feasibility of collection; (3) the effect of alternative levels of demand on the three basic pricing problems (when marginal costs are less than, equal to, or exceed average costs); (4) distinguishing between several types of price discrimination and related practices such as peak load pricing; (5) a summary of results of recent studies of user fee policies in public agencies; and (6) the implications for improving future fee practices.

C. Visitor Response to Price and Price Changes

These authors suggest that consumer input, rather than management assumptions, should serve as the essential guide in determining prices. A better understanding of who visitors are may help managers anticipate reactions to fees and help guide the development of appropriate pricing policies. These studies also concluded that: (1) visitors react differently to prices charged for different activities; (2) price expectations and reactions to price can be influenced by information campaigns; and (3) expectations of visitors may continue to heighten over time, leading to more fee increases.

Howard, Dennis R.; Selin, Steven W. 1987. A method for establishing consumer price tolerance levels for public recreation services. Journal of Park and Recreation Administration. 5(3): 48–59.

Annotation: See section IV.A. page 11.

McCarville, Ronald E. 1990. The role of cognitive processes in explaining reactions to price changes for leisure services. Journal of Park and Recreation Administration. 8(3): 74–86.

Annotation: This paper compares and contrasts the traditional rationalist model of the price/demand relationship with an information-processing or cognitive model. Both approaches offer insights that facilitate the development of effective pricing strategies. The rationalist model assumes an inverse relationship between demand and price. The information processing perspective assumes that price-related stimuli are interpreted, manipulated, and assessed in such a way that rising prices may not lead to decreased demand. Information acquisition and evaluation is discussed in relation to a suggested theoretical framework, which reflects the often reciprocal relationship between information acquisition and expectation. Comparative price information may contribute to price elasticity by moving perceptual price anchors or expectations closer to new price levels, thus influencing the acceptability of new price levels. Administrative actions that can influence response to price increases and subsequent demand for services are suggested.

McDonald, Cary D.; Noe, Frank P.; Hammitt, William E. 1987. Expectations and recreation fees: a dilemma for recreation resource administrators. Journal of Park and Recreation Administration. 5(2): 1–9.

Annotation: An expanded fee program may have negative consequences for administrators if visitors expect more benefits as fees increase. Exchange theory logic and cost-benefit analysis was used to examine the hypothesis that the amount of money an individual would be willing to pay is positively related to the desire for additional services. More than 300 visitors completed a mail questionnaire during spring 1984 at the Big South Fork National River and Recreation Area in Tennessee. The survey assessed willingness to pay and preference for development. A weak relationship between willingness to pay and preference for development was found only for visitors in the high fee group (visitors willing to pay $5 or more). Administrators may be able to charge a low to moderate fee without visitors desiring additional benefits.

More, Thomas A.; Dustin, Daniel L.; Knopf, Richard C. 1996. Behavioral consequences of campground user fees. Journal of Park and Recreation Administration. 14(1): 81–93.

Annotation: Not all implications of fees are fully understood. This study examines the effects of price on campers' expectations and examines the influence of price on campers' perception of appropriate behavior. Using telephone interviews, 910 campers who had applied for a campground reservation at any Forest Service campground in California between January 1991 and May 1992 were contacted. Interview topics consisted of general attitudes toward fees, attitudes about camping in general, campground attributes and appropriate camping behaviors, and socioeconomic data. Most subjects (73 percent) felt that fees charged at public campsites were about right, although 20 percent felt that current fees were too high. In addition, 85 percent felt that campgrounds should be financed with a combination of tax dollars and use fees, with 31 percent preferring a 50-50 match. Respondents were willing to pay a mean of $8.19 for a primitive campground, and $16.27 for a developed campground with services such as showers, electricity, and a small store. Although in this study fee increases were not related to a change in what behaviors are acceptable at campgrounds, there was a relationship between price and expectations. If fee increases prompt heightened expectations for facilities and services, it may lead to a spiral where more fee increases are needed to continue satisfying those heightened expectations.

D. Determining or Altering Visitor/ Consumer Price Expectations

These studies show that consumer price expectations and willingness-to-pay levels can be influenced by cost-of-service information and prices paid previously.

Kyle, Gerard T.; Kerstetter, Deborah L.; Guadagnolo, Frank B. 1999. The influence of outcome messages and involvement on participant reference price. Journal of Park and Recreation Administration. 17(3): 53–75.

Annotation: The primary purpose of this study was to examine methods of manipulating consumers' internal reference price (IRP) for a 10K road race offered by a public recreation agency. A secondary purpose was to examine the relationship between runners' level of involvement and their IRP. A total of 468 subjects, drawn from a systematic sample of competitors who entered in the race, were systematically assigned to one of six treatment groups. Each subject received a message communicating potential outcomes associated with paying an entrance fee for a 10K road race. Subsequent changes in subjects' IRP were monitored. The results indicated that cost of service information was the most effective treatment message in encouraging significantly higher IRP. In addition, as the subjects' level of social psychological involvement with running increased, so too did their IRP. However, as past participation in the event increased, their internal reference price decreased. These findings indicate that managers of public leisure services do have the ability to manipulate consumers' price expectations for the services they provide.

McCarville, Ronald E. 1996. The importance of price last paid in developing price expectations for a public leisure service. Journal of Park and Recreation Administration. 14(4): 52–64.

Annotation: Though fees may generate needed revenues for various initiatives, fees and charges may also provoke negative reactions among users. This paper examines the psycho-

logical importance of price last paid in determining recreation participants' price. Users of a community indoor swimming pool were asked to complete a written survey while visiting the pool. Survey questions included current use patterns, perceived quality of the facility, attachment to the swim complex, what respondents would expect to pay for admission, and sociodemographic items. A total of 109 visitors completed the survey. Results show that price last paid was critical to the establishment of price expectations for the respondents who participated in open swims and lane swimming. Price last paid seemed relatively unimportant to those who participated in aquatic fitness classes or had children registered in swim classes. The importance of price last paid seems grounded in previous exposure to price levels, the cumulative effect of repeated fee payments, and even knowledge of prices charged by competing providers. Management implications include using fee discount programs to encourage greater behavioral loyalty to the facility, and making a clear distinction between the "regular" prices charged at other facilities and the discount price.

McCarville, Ronald E. 1997. The anchoring effect of price-last-paid information on willingness-to-pay levels. Journal of Applied Recreation Research. 22(3): 191–209.

Annotation: See section V.B. page 16.

McCarville, Ronald E.; Crompton, John L. 1987. Propositions addressing perceptions of reference price for public recreation services. Leisure Sciences. 9(4): 281–291.

Annotation: This paper reviews literature relating to consumers' perceptions of reference price. Nine propositions are suggested as a result of the literature review and are grouped under three headings: (1) the roles of perception and reference price; (2) the influence of information on reference price; and (3) the role of equity in reference to price perception. The intent is to provide a framework for discussion and stimulate future research into understanding the role of reference prices in the context of public recreation services.

McCarville, Ronald E.; Crompton, John L.; Sell, Jane A. 1993. The influence of outcome messages on reference prices. Leisure Sciences. 15: 115–130.

Annotation: This study examined the effects of messages describing alternative potential outcomes for a hypothetical aerobics program on the development of higher price expectations. The potential outcomes included a change in program cost, the possibility of losing the program, taking money from another program due to inadequate fee revenues to cover costs, or using excess fees to improve the program. A total of 224 undergraduate sociology students were randomly assigned to one of six treatment groups, with each group receiving a different outcome message. Results show that respondents were particularly responsive to the message suggesting that other participants would suffer if sufficient revenues from fees to meet program costs were not generated. The mean reference price (what they expected to pay) reported by this group was 41 percent greater than other groups. Level of involvement toward aerobic activity was found to influence price expectations, current activity patterns, and intent to enroll in future aerobics programs.

V. WILLINGNESS TO PAY (WTP) AND RECREATION FEES

A. WTP as a Tool to Develop Fee Programs

Monetary values for outdoor recreation resources and experiences are often measured using contingent valuation methods. One such method is willingness to pay (WTP). Although there are different ways of measuring WTP, it is commonly measured with a survey question, such as: "Would you be willing to pay $X for a day use fee at the Desolation Wilderness?" WTP information can be used to evaluate whether revenues from a specific fee program could support a recreation program. For example, WTP information can be used to determine a potential entrance fee amount, and to determine potential consequences of fees on visitation demand. While WTP surveys can be used to evaluate fee programs, they must be carefully designed to include measures of fee acceptance, behavioral response to fees, and alternative pricing options. One study found that satisfied customers would be willing to pay higher fees putting more pressure on management to make satisfactory experiences available to the visitor. It is important to note that WTP studies are often hypothetical; peoples' actual behaviors may differ from their responses to hypothetical scenarios.

Adams, R. M.; Bergland, O.; Musser, W. N.; Johnson, S. L.; Musser, L. M. 1989. User fees and equity issues in public hunting expenditures: The case of ring-necked pheasant in Oregon. Land Economics. 65(4): 376–385.

Annotation: This study investigated economic aspects of implementing user fees for a public game enhancement program for ring-necked pheasants in Oregon. Due to increasing costs, the Oregon Department of Fish and Wildlife decided to eliminate the pheasant propagation and stocking program. A user-supported program involving access fees was suggested as a means to continue the program. The analysis is based on a closed-form contingent valuation survey of 97 hunters during the 1986 western Oregon pheasant season. Contingent valuation methods were used to elicit hunter willingness to pay estimates for the continuation of the pheasant-stocking program. These estimates were used to generate information on the likelihood that a user fee system could maintain such a

program. Results suggest that the program is an efficient expenditure of public funds, with a surplus of $49,000. However, a revenue-maximizing fee of $14 per hunter per season would not generate sufficient expenditures to support the program because of substantial decline in participation among lower income groups.

Berrens, Robert P.; Adams, Richard M. 1998. Applying contingent valuation in the design of fee hunting programs: pheasant hunting in Oregon revisited. Human Dimensions of Wildlife. 3(3): 11–25.

Annotation: The feasibility of user fees to support a public stocking program for pheasant hunting at the E. E. Wilson Wildlife Area in western Oregon was initially evaluated in 1989 using a survey-based contingent valuation (CV) method. Subsequent to this survey, an experimental "put and take" stocking program was conducted at the site. Several fee levels were charged for hunting pheasants. Application of the CV method to investigate potential fee hunting at this Wildlife Area is used as an illustrative case study to evaluate the performance of the original study and ask how CV may be used in designing and evaluating pricing policies for revenue capture in fee hunting programs. For future fee hunting studies, the authors suggest that contingent behavior questions supplement standard contingent valuation questions. Survey design needs to be directed not only to acceptance rates of alternative fees, but also to expected behavioral responses to alternative pricing policies (such as changes in length of stay, or switching to alternative sites). To be a pragmatic tool in evaluating hunters' willingness to pay and the potential for user fees to generate revenues, survey designs must accommodate alternative pricing policies.

McDonald, Cary D.; Hammitt, William E.; Dottavio, F. Dominic. 1985. An individual's willingness to pay for a river visit. In: Popadic, Joseph S.; Butterfield, Dorothy I.; Anderson, Dorothy H.; Popadic, Mary R., eds. 1984 National river recreation symposium proceedings; 1984 October 31–November 3; Baton Rouge, LA. Baton Rouge: Louisiana State University: 605–618.

Annotation: The hypothetical market approach (also called contingent valuation) was used to determine an individual's willingness to pay for an entry fee per river visit at the Big South Fork National River and Recreation Area in Tennessee. On the average, individuals were willing to pay $4.21 per visit, with the willingness to pay value ranging from $0 to $25. About one-fifth (22 percent) of respondents were not willing to pay any fee. Of the variables age, education, income, distance traveled, past visitation, number of rivers floated, and attitude toward fees, income was the only variable not related to willingness to pay. The two most important explanatory variables were number of rivers floated and attitude toward fees.

McDonald, Cary D.; Noe, Frank P.; Hammitt, William E. 1987. Expectations and recreation fees: a dilemma for recreation resource administrators. Journal of Park and Recreation Administration. 5(2): 1–9.

Annotation: See section IV.C. page 13.

Noe, Francis P.; McDonald, Cary D.; Hammitt, William E. 1986. Exchange satisfaction for fees: Willingness to pay for a park environment. Journal of Environmental Systems. 16(2): 111–122.

Annotation: Instituting a user fee policy may change role relations between visitors and management. It may also change visitor expectations toward programs, facilities, and services, and increase the real potential for adversary confrontations. This paper evaluates the merit of charging a fee by measuring an individual's level of satisfaction and possible unintended consequences associated with their willingness to pay. Two hypotheses are tested: (1) satisfied visitors would be unwilling to pay more in return for what they already have received and found satisfying; and (2) satisfied visitors would be willing to provide support for a continued satisfying experience by spending a higher dollar amount. A whitewater river study, a rafting study, and a deer hunter study were used to test these two hypotheses. The social exchange model used in analysis found support for the argument that if park visitors are highly satisfied, they will be willing to pay more for a park experience.

B. Exploring the Meaning of WTP Levels

These authors explore the meanings (economic, personal, and others) that may be reflected in willingness-to-pay levels reported by the public. For example, willingness-to-pay levels emerge from a complex mix of moral considerations, emotional experiences, activity involvement, and price last paid. However, willingness-to-pay levels may not adequately express spiritual and intrinsic values of a wilderness experience.

Ajzen, Icek; Driver, B. L. 1992. Contingent value measurement: on the nature and meaning of willingness to pay. Journal of Consumer Psychology. 1(4): 297–316.

Annotation: The meaning of contingent valuation measures for five outdoor activities was explored using the theory of planned behavior. This theory treats willingness to pay for public goods as a behavioral intention. To assign dollar values to goods that are not traded in the marketplace, survey participants could: (1) rely on their experience with or knowledge about such transactions; or (2) in the absence of directly relevant information, they could base their judgments on intuitive guidelines or rules of thumb. Participants in the

questionnaire consisted of 150 undergraduate students representing a broad range of liberal arts and social science majors. Analysis showed that the perceived effect (desirable consequences) of the activity, and ethical and moral considerations were predictive of willingness to pay a user fee. Normative expectations and available resources also added to moral considerations in determining how much money one would be willing to pay. Overall, this shows that respondents appear to use intuitive guidelines to make their judgments. These findings indicate that willingness-to-pay judgments may reflect only some, and not necessarily the most important, variables that would be expected to influence these judgments.

McCarville, Ronald E. 1997. The anchoring effect of price-last-paid information on willingness-to-pay levels. Journal of Applied Recreation Research. 22(3): 191–209.

Annotation: This study monitored whether willingness-to-pay levels could be influenced by psychological reference points. An experimental format placed participants in a hypothetical recreation day-use area and used a series of photographic slides to simulate this setting. Respondents were offered hypothetical messages offering various "price-last-paid" levels and were asked to report their willingness-to-pay levels for entry into this hypothetical site. The control group received no price-last-paid information, the second group was asked to assume they had paid a $2 admission fee on the last visit, and the third group was told they had previously paid $4. Willingness-to-pay levels for admission to the site were increased by as much as 41 percent by these messages. It seems that the values participants report for public leisure services may be influenced by memories of prices paid during previous visits to similar sites.

Trainor, Sarah Fleisher; Norgaard, Richard B. 1999. Recreation fees in the context of wilderness values. Journal of Park and Recreation Administration. 17(3): 100–115.

Annotation: This research investigates the relationship between statements of willingness-to-pay fees for wilderness use and descriptions of spiritual and intrinsic wilderness values. Specifically, the research sought to understand if, in the mind of the wilderness user, spiritual and intrinsic values are adequately reflected in statements of willingness to pay fees. Data were collected via standardized, semistructured interviews with 100 day or overnight Desolation Wilderness users in July 1997. The interviews were designed to learn how people think of three forms of wilderness value (economic, spiritual, and intrinsic) and the relationships between them. Study participants largely supported wilderness use fees. Findings show the possibility of simultaneous pragmatic support for wilderness fees and conceptual disapproval of treating the wilderness as a commodity. When expressions of economic value were compared to those of spiritual and intrinsic values, the majority of respondents found monetary willingness to pay bids an inadequate expression of spiritual and intrinsic values. These results indicate a need for further research regarding the relationships between willingness to pay and multiple wilderness values so that the design and implementation of wilderness fee programs can achieve cost recovery without offending users who disapprove of commodifying the wilderness resource.

VI. ATTITUDES TOWARD RECREATION FEES

A. Identifying Attitudes Toward Fees

These studies suggest that, in general, the majority of the general public, hikers, and fee program managers surveyed support fees rather than oppose them. Few perceived negative impacts from fees were reported.

Bowker, J. M.; Cordell, H. K.; Johnson, Cassandra Y. 1999. User fees for recreation services on public lands: a national assessment. Journal of Park and Recreation Administration. 17(3): 1–14.

Annotation: This research contributes to a previously unexplored niche in the user fee debate by reporting on national sentiment toward user fees for outdoor recreation services. Data on public opinion regarding the implementation of user fees to fully or partially fund 10 broad categories of wilderness and nonwilderness recreation services on public land was obtained from the 1995 National Survey on Recreation and the Environment. Additionally, regression models were used to test the effects of various sociodemographic factors in explaining support for user fees. Respondents were offered five choices to fund these services including fees only, fees and taxes, taxes only, don't provide the service, and don't know. Boat ramps, campgrounds, and special exhibits drew the most support for user fees. However, for six of the 10 recreation services examined (visitor centers, trails, picnic areas, restrooms, parking areas, and historic sites) there was more support for funding from taxes only than from fees or a combination of fees and taxes. In some of the models discussed, income and ethnicity surfaced as significant exploratory variables. A number of regional differences also emerged indicating differing levels of support for user fees around the country.

Economics Research Associates. 1976. Evaluation of public willingness to pay user charges for use of outdoor recreation areas and facilities. Prepared for: U.S. Department of the Interior, Bureau of Outdoor Recreation, Washington, DC. 024-016-00087-1. 45 p.

Annotation: The Bureau of Outdoor Recreation authorized this study to develop base data on fee policies of government agencies, fee levels in comparable public and private areas, and public willingness to pay for recreation services. Data were collected from a national citizen survey of 800 households, interviews with State, local, and Federal recreation administrators, interviews with 240 State, city, and county recreation departments, and interviews with representatives of private recreation areas. Many respondents (52 to 76 percent, depending on the demographic group) felt recreation services should be on more of a pay-as-you-go basis. The greatest support for pay-as-you-go fees came from the elderly, the lower income groups, and rural residents, which often corresponded to persons with lower rates of recreation participation. Generally, participants would also be willing to pay significantly higher user fees at public areas for all activities. Respondents felt that 52 percent of fee revenues should contribute to special facilities, 47 percent to operations and maintenance, and 33 percent to land acquisition. An entrance fee was heavily favored (76 percent) over activity fees (24 percent). Considerably more city and county recreation administrators felt that users should not pay for outdoor recreation activities (21 and 25 percent, respectively) than State administrators (3 percent). Administrators felt that public reaction to fees was generally one of approval or acceptance. Administrators frequently commented that fees should be one of a group of funding sources, rather than the primary source.

Fedler, Anthony J.; Miles, Ann F. 1989. Paying for backcountry recreation: understanding the acceptability of use fees. Journal of Park and Recreation Administration. 7(2): 35–46.

Annotation: This study identified hiker attitudes toward use fees and determined which combination of overall attitude toward use fees and type of fee, amount of fee, or willingness to pay is effective to assess various fee implementation alternatives. A random sample of 100 hikers from Great Smokey Mountain National Park, Linville Gorge Wilderness Area, and Grandfather Mountain were sent mail surveys. Approximately one-third of respondents favored fees and one-third opposed fees. Although hikers preferred to pay by voluntary contribution, they were willing to pay $1 to $2 for a daily fee and $5 to $10 for an annual permit. Some willingness to pay amounts increased if the revenue was returned directly to the local site. The majority of hikers also indicated they would be willing to pay fees to participate in other backcountry recreation activities.

Krannich, Richard S.; Eisenhauer, Brian W.; Field, Donald R.; Pratt, Cristina; Luloff, A. E. 1999. Implications of the National Park Service Recreational Fee Demonstration Program for park operations and management: perceptions of NPS managers. Journal of Park and Recreation Administration. 17(3): 35–52.

Annotation: This study examines the insights of onsite managers regarding their perceived effects of the Recreational Fee Demonstration Program. The analysis includes results of a mail survey of administrative personnel responsible for Fee Demonstration Program management at 109 National Park Service units that were participating in the program in 1997. Results indicate that managers generally have positive perceptions of the program and its effects. Very few of these managers perceived negative effects on visitation, and most reported that the responses of local and nonlocal visitors have been either positive or neutral. About one-fourth of the managers indicated problems with program administration that they perceived as originating at the local-unit level, and a similar number perceived problems as originating from regional-level administration. Nearly half perceived problems attributed to national-level National Park Service administration. Examination of variables reflecting varying park contexts indicates that perceptions of program effects are associated with differences in visitation levels and patterns, unit type, and regional location. These differences suggest that a "one size fits all" program, while easier to administer, may be less effective in meeting on-the-ground needs.

Schneider, Ingrid; LaPointe, Christopher; Stievater, Sharon. 2000. Perceptions of and preferences for fee program dollar utilization among wilderness visitors. In: Cole, David N.; McCool, Stephen F.; Borrie, William T.; O'Loughlin, Jennifer, comps. Wilderness science in a time of change conference—Volume 4: Wilderness visitors, experiences, and visitor management; 1999 May 23–27; Missoula, MT. Proc. RMRS-P-15-VOL-4. Ogden, UT: U.S. Department of Agriculture, Forest Service, Rocky Mountain Research Station: 164–166.

Annotation: Visitors to the Superstition Wilderness in Arizona were surveyed to determine demographics, activity, activity style, perceptions of the fee program, and preferences for use of funds collected. At the time of the survey, a $4 self-pay fee was charged at the wilderness' two main trailheads. Approximately 45 percent of the respondents were knowledgeable about the fee program and 56 percent agreed they understood the reasons behind it. Knowledge and perception of the fee program was more related to activity style (in other words, the various personal meanings assigned to an activity by an individual) than to activity, indicating a more precise technique for managers to use in future surveys. Most (79.7 percent) respondents agreed that the fee would not affect their visitation, and many (42.7 percent) agreed that it might limit access for some people. This study did not consider the visitors who were already displaced. Visitors had relatively high incomes and were already being charged for entry, which may have minimized the effects of the fee.

Winter, Patricia L.; Palucki, Laura J. 1999. Anticipated responses to a fee program: the key is trust. Journal of Leisure Research. 31(3): 207–226.

Annotation: See section VI.B. page 19.

B. Influences on Attitudes Toward Fees

These studies showed that acceptability of fees can be influenced by a variety of factors including public trust, past fee-paying experience, price, past wilderness experience, and how the fee is used by the managing agency.

Anderson, Kristin H. 2000. The debate surrounding newly implemented recreation user fees on Federal lands: an examination of those actively opposed. Missoula, MT: The University of Montana. 120 p. Thesis.

Annotation: See section III. page 9.

Bowker, J. M.; Cordell, H. K.; Johnson, Cassandra Y. 1999. User fees for recreation services on public lands: a national assessment. Journal of Park and Recreation Administration. 17(3): 1–14.

Annotation: See section VI.A. page 17.

Kerr, Geoff N.; Manfredo, Michael J. 1991. An attitudinal based model of pricing for recreation services. Journal of Leisure Research. 23(1): 37–50.

Annotation: An attitudinal model of pricing is tested for the ability to predict acceptance of paying fees, and explain the basis for people's tolerances. The model proposes that attitudes and past behavior are the primary determinants of fee-paying intentions. Study participants were sampled from recreationists who used backcountry huts in New Zealand's Arthur's Pass National Park and Tararua Forest Park. Recreationists were contacted in 1988 using trailhead interviews. A total of 437 usable questionnaires were obtained. Items on the survey measured responses to belief statements about proposed fee levels at huts, paying intentions, past use, and past paying experience. Price was found to have no direct impact on intentions to pay fees but had a strong indirect impact via attitude. This supports the hypothesis that price information is used in determining attitude toward fee paying intentions. The model can be a useful prediction tool in making pricing decisions, and provide useful information in developing pricing strategies that incorporate information programs to mediate the negative reactions to fee increases.

Leuschner, William A.; Cook, Philip S.; Roggenbuck, Joseph W.; Oderwald, Richard G. 1987. A comparative analysis for wilderness user fee policy. Journal of Leisure Research. 19(2): 101–114.

Annotation: See section VII.A. page 22.

McCarville, Ronald E.; Reiling, Stephen D.; White, Christopher M. 1996. The role of fairness in users' assessments of first-time fees for a public recreation service. Leisure Sciences. 18: 61–76.

Annotation: This paper examines the effects of past experience with paying fees, level of service, and users' proximity to sites on possible displacement and perceptions of fairness of fees for day-use recreation areas. Six U.S. Army Corps of Engineers day-use areas were selected. A mail survey of 1,405 visitors to these areas suggests the presence of two client types. The first type had paid fees in the past and seemed relatively less troubled by the prospect of doing so again in the future. In all cases, this group was more willing to pay fees and to pay higher fee levels than its counterpart. The second type typically had not paid fees for public leisure services, and its members resent even the implication that they may be asked to do so. They assert that fees are unfair and that they feel victimized through the introduction of fees. User resentment is exacerbated by participants' familiarity with the recreational setting. Those living closest to the sites are most likely to be indignant at the thought of paying a first-time fee.

Reiling, Stephen D.; Criner, George K.; Oltmanns, Steven E. 1988. The influence of information on users' attitudes toward campground user fees. Journal of Leisure Research. 20(3): 208–217.

Annotation: To determine whether an educational program can alter users' attitudes about fees, resident and nonresident visitors of Maine State park campgrounds were surveyed in 1984. Just over 700 completed mail surveys were obtained. Respondents were asked to indicate whether the current fee of $5 per site per night for a campsite was too high, too low, or about right in three scenarios. Each scenario provided different information about other fees and costs. The first scenario offered no additional information. The second asked them to rate the current fee with the knowledge that the average fee at commercial campgrounds was $8. The third scenario informed respondents that it actually cost the Maine Bureau of Parks and Recreation about $11 per site per night to provide a State park campsite. After receiving the information, respondents were asked to rate the current fee of $5 again. Results for the first scenario show that the majority (87 percent) of Maine residents felt that the current fee was about right. After being provided with the information in the second scenario, Maine residents who felt the current fee was too low went up from 9 to 14 percent. And again, after the third scenario, that percentage went up from 14 to 38 percent. Similar results are reported for nonresidents of Maine. These results suggest that an information program may be an effective way to improve the willingness of users to accept a fee increase.

Williams, Daniel R.; Vogt, Christine A.; Vitterso, Joar. 1999. Structural equation modeling of users' response to wilderness recreation fees. Journal of Leisure Research. 31(3): 245–268.

Annotation: In the case of wilderness recreation fees, it is important to recognize the complex public purpose of wilderness and the long history of not having access fees in wilderness. To evaluate these various factors, this paper examines the impact of past wilderness experience and residential proximity on response to wilderness use fees using a structural equation approach. Data came from the 1997 survey of Desolation Wilderness overnight visitors who paid a fee. Findings suggest wilderness users generally support fees for public recreation, but fees are judged to be less appropriate for wilderness than for more developed recreation facilities and services. Structural equation modeling shows that experienced wilderness users, experienced Desolation Wilderness users, and users residing in proximity to the Desolation Wilderness are less

supportive of fees and less likely to see positive benefits from fees. A history of paying fees for access to other recreation sites and perceptions of wilderness problems, though positively related to past wilderness experience, do not contribute to fee support.

Winter, Patricia L.; Palucki, Laura J. 1999. Anticipated responses to a fee program: the key is trust. Journal of Leisure Research. 31(3): 207–226.

Annotation: The primary objective of this study was to describe anticipated reactions to a proposed fee program in southern California National Forests prior to its implementation. Focus groups and a questionnaire examined social trust's relationship to perceived fairness of the fee program (defined in terms of anticipated impacts to self and others), general attitudes toward the program (such as thinking the program was a good thing), and amounts people were willing to pay for the recreation pass. Trust's relationship to these variables was expected to vary by communities of interest (based on ethnicity and recreation activity groups) and communities of place (based on residency within a National Forest boundary and greater geographic proximity). Conditional acceptance, and in some cases, outright disapproval, were expressed during the group discussions. Social trust was revealed as the only significant contributor to explaining the variance (more than 38 percent) in anticipated impacts and general opinions about fees.

VII. Influences of Recreation Fees on Visitation and Use

A. Effects of Fees on Use

Research findings in this category generally show that fees have negative effects on use patterns. Differential fees (for example, higher fees at popular sites or during peak periods and/or lower fees at other sites or times) may not be an income-neutral use rationing method. Low-income visitor groups can be more sensitive to price changes and are more likely to be priced out of a recreation site or activity. In addition, these studies document that fees have caused displacement as well as changes in frequency and length of visit.

Bamford, Tara E.; Manning, Robert E.; Forcier, Lawrence K.; Koenemann, Edward J. 1988. Differential campsite pricing: an experiment. Journal of Leisure Research. 20(4): 324–342.

Annotation: To test the effectiveness of differential pricing on altering use patterns, a differential pricing system was implemented at campsites in 14 Vermont State parks. Upon arrival at the campground, campers were given a map showing the sites and their costs. Campers' site choices were recorded, and their names and addresses were obtained from campsite receipts. Half of the sample was also mailed a questionnaire to gather socioeconomic and attitudinal data. Results show that the "prime" (most popular) campsites experienced a decreased occupancy rate. Generally, campground use was more evenly distributed, and there was an increase in revenues. Families with higher incomes were more likely to select prime campsites (which are higher cost). Lower income campers were less satisfied with the camping fee, tended to be less favorably inclined toward the concept of fee differentials and the size of the differentials, and tended to consider price more important in the campsite selection process. Care should be taken in implementing and monitoring new pricing policies because they can alter recreation participation patterns.

Bowker, J. M.; Leeworthy, V. R. 1998. Accounting for ethnicity in recreation demand: a flexible count data approach. Journal of Leisure Research. 30(1): 64–78.

Annotation: Little research exists that incorporates cultural differences into demand models explaining trip-taking behavior. This paper examines ethnicity and individual trip-taking behavior associated with natural resource-based recreation in the Florida Keys. The travel cost method is used to estimate trip demand. Interviews with people at a variety of different sites, including hotels, campgrounds, and museums, were conducted in July and August 1995. Results show that Hispanics are more sensitive to price changes, and that increased travel costs, resulting from increases in entry or access fees, could result in the Hispanic population being priced out of the market.

Kerkvliet, Joe; Nowell, Clifford. 2000. Tools for recreation management in parks: the case of the greater Yellowstone's blue-ribbon fishery. Ecological Economics. 34: 89–100.

Annotation: Although this paper primarily developed statistical models to examine a broad range of management tools, it also addressed the potential impacts of fees on recreation use. The authors developed models explaining site choice and visitation based on surveys of anglers in the Greater Yellowstone Ecosystem. Respondents were predominantly Caucasian, well educated, and wealthy (modal response for income level was greater than $100,000). Despite the relatively high income of respondents, the authors found that increases in site-specific daily fees would reduce the number of days anglers visited a site. Alternatively, increases in seasonal permit costs (not related to sites) had little affect on fishing pressure. Therefore, they concluded that if management goals were to reduce ecological impact, site-specific fees might function more effectively. Because increased seasonal permit costs functioned to increase trip length (and thus did not help to alleviate use), this tool may be effective if managers were trying to pursue revenue goals.

Leuschner, William A.; Cook, Philip S.; Roggenbuck, Joseph W.; Oderwald, Richard G. 1987. A comparative analysis for wilderness user fee policy. Journal of Leisure Research. 19(2): 101–114.

Annotation: Party leaders at the Linville Gorge Wilderness (nonfee) and the Grandfather Mountain backcountry area (a privately owned fee area) were sent mail surveys during the summer season in 1985. Survey topics included user characteristics, trip characteristics, fees, and travel cost method (TCM). TCM is a method of estimating recreation site demand by using travel cost from the visitor's residence to the recreation site. User characteristics, trip characteristics, and TCM data all indicated that fees did not cause a difference between populations or trip behavior. Responses indicated that users would rather not pay fees than pay them, but that behavior and use patterns would not be drastically altered if fees were implemented. Fees are more strongly supported by those already paying them but are strongly supported by both groups if paying fees will prevent deterioration of wilderness areas. The authors conclude that these results make a strong case for consideration of a wilderness fee system.

Lindberg, Kreg; Aylward, Bruce. 1999. Price responsiveness in the developing country nature tourism context: review and Costa Rican case study. Journal of Leisure Research. 31(3): 281–299.

Annotation: The United States is not alone in considering and implementing visitor fees. Evaluations of international experience are uncommon in the recreation literature, and much of the research has focused on valuation rather than price responsiveness. This article reviews estimates of willingness to pay, revenue maximizing fees, and price elasticities in developing countries. It then uses actual price and visitation data to estimate price elasticities for three National Parks in Costa Rica. The results clearly indicate price inelasticity of demand at fee levels up to and beyond $10, indicating that revenue at these three National Parks may be increased significantly by raising fee levels with (relatively) little effect on visitation levels.

Manning, Robert E.; Callinan, Elaine A.; Echelberger, Herbert E.; Koenemann, Edward J.; McEwen, Douglas N. 1984. Differential fees: raising revenue, distributing demand. Journal of Parks and Recreation Administration. 2(1): 20–38.

Annotation: To determine the extent to which differential fees would influence campsite selection patterns, a range of differential fees based on campsite popularity was assigned at three Vermont State parks. Campers had knowledge of the differential costs of campsites before they chose one and paid for it. Campsite receipts from August 1982 were used to collect selection data and to obtain addresses to send questionnaires to campers. The questionnaires collected data on their camping visit, experience and equipment, level of satisfaction with the park experience, socioeconomic characteristics, and the importance of price in selecting a campsite. The findings suggest that the differential fee system did cause a small but statistically significant shift in campsite selection patterns from more heavily used to less-used sites. No socioeconomic or other discriminatory effects were found as a result of the differential fee system.

Marsinko, Allan. 2000. The effect of fees on recreation site choice: management/agency implications. In: Proceedings of the 1999 Northeastern Recreation Research Symposium, 1999 April 11–14; The Sagamore on Lake George in Bolton Landing, New York. Gen. Tech. Rep. NE 269. Newton Square, PA: U.S. Department of Agriculture, Forest Service, Northeastern Research Station: 164–171.

Annotation: This descriptive study used visitor use patterns and interviews to explore possible visitor responses to recreation fees. Specifically, day-use visitors were surveyed to determine whether fees affect their choice of recreation site. The author interviewed visitors at seven recreation sites in South Carolina, only some of which charged fees. Most respondents had little knowledge of the managing agency or other nearby sites. Although respondents considered the cost of entry fees, cost did not limit the choice of sites used. Instead, crowding was the major reason that caused users to switch sites. The pattern observed may have resulted from users settling at recreation sites where they already felt comfortable with the fee amount (no fee in some cases) and the level of crowding.

More, Thomas; Stevens, Thomas. 2000. Do user fees exclude low-income people from resource-based recreation? Journal of Leisure Research. 32(3): 341–357.

Annotation: Past research has generally focused on surveys conducted at recreation sites after the decision to recreate had already been made. The authors of this study conducted a mail survey that was based on census data to make sure they procured responses of low-income households. Respondents were divided into low-, middle-, and high-income groups. Based on their survey results, the authors concluded that fees discriminated against low-income people. A total of 23 percent of low-income households indicated they had already reduced or changed their recreation activity in response to fees (compared to 11 percent of high-income households). In addition, 49 percent of low-income people said that a $5 fee would affect their future participation in activities compared to 37 percent and 33 percent of middle- and high-income households, respectively. Low-income households generally planned to participate in activities less than middle- or high-income households. Low-income households were more likely than other income groups to prefer donations to fees as a means of fundraising and to indicate that "all taxpayers" should pay to maintain and improve parks and forests. The authors suggested that serious policy questions are raised about the purpose of public recreation when potential user groups are excluded.

Reiling, Stephen; Cheng, Hsiang-tai; Robinson, Chris; McCarville, Ronald; White, Christopher. 1996. Potential equity effects of a new day-use fee. In: Dawson, Chad P., comp. Proceedings of the 1995 Northeastern recreation research symposium; 1995 April 9–11; Saratoga Springs, NY. Gen. Tech. Rep. NE-218. Radnor, PA: U.S. Department of Agriculture, Forest Service, Northeastern Forest Experiment Station. 27–31.

Annotation: During the summer of 1993, visitors to 18 Army Corps of Engineers day-use sites were surveyed to determine their attitudes toward fees and how they would respond to a day-use fee. A major objective of the study was to determine whether low-income users would be displaced. Questionnaire items were aimed at determining how current users would respond to a fee system and the number of trips they would make to the day-use area at alternative fee levels. A total of 1,405 surveys were completed and returned. A comparison of users who indicated they were not willing to pay any fee (40 percent) and those who were willing to pay a fee showed that low-income users have a higher probability of choosing to not pay a fee, thereby terminating their use of the day-use sites at a greater rate than current users with higher levels of income. Results also show that low-income users who were willing to pay a fee are much more sensitive to the size of the fee.

Reiling, Stephen D.; Cheng, Hsiang-tai; Trott, Cheryl. 1992. Measuring the discriminatory impact associated with higher recreational fees. Leisure Sciences. 14: 121–137.

Annotation: This article presents an approach for determining whether higher fees may cause low-income users to reduce their use of outdoor facilities. Data were obtained from a random sample of 1,066 users of Maine State park campgrounds during 1984. The mail survey gathered data on actual camping behavior (number of nights camped), and used open-ended contingent valuation questions to determine if there would be a change in the number of nights camped at campgrounds with higher fee levels. The approach in this paper uses the estimated demand for camping at Maine State parks to empirically show that campers will respond differently to higher fees depending on their level of income. Specifically, low-income campers would reduce their camping activity.

Schneider, Ingrid E.; Budruk, Megha. 1999. Displacement as a response to the Federal recreation fee program. Journal of Park and Recreation Administration. 17(3): 76–84.

Annotation: One potential criticism of fees and fee programs is their possibility of displacing current visitors. However, due to the challenging nature and additional resources required to study and understand displaced visitors, few studies include visitors who are actually displaced. The purpose of this study was: (1) to ascertain behavioral changes due to the fee program ranging from displacement to visit composition changes (frequency, length, and so forth), and (2) to determine if displaced visitors hold more negative perceptions of the fee program. Visitors to a nonfee area within a National Forest were surveyed to ascertain visitor responses and displacement from the fee areas in other parts of the forest. A total of 346 responses were obtained. Results indicated one-half of respondents chose the site because it was free and that one-third of visitors had changed their visitation in response to the fee program. Of the visitors who changed their behavior, one-half indicated intersite or intrasite displacement, and 70 percent indicated they visit less frequently. Displacement appears to be a consequence of the fee program. It is possible that better and more persuasive information related to the fee program may diminish the number of people it displaces.

Schroeder, Herbert W.; Louviere, Jordan. 1999. Stated choice models for predicting the impact of user fees at public recreation sites. Journal of Leisure Research. 31(3): 300–324.

Annotation: A crucial question in the implementation of fee programs is how the users of recreation sites will respond to various levels and types of fees. Stated choice models can help managers anticipate the impact of user fees on people's choices among the alternative recreation sites available to them. Two models are presented in this paper to illustrate how stated choice models can help assess the impact of fee changes on the likelihood of choosing a site, and the importance of fees relative to other site attributes in people's choices. One model is based on a 1986 telephone and mail survey of Chicago-area residents, and the other is based on a two-phase mail survey concerning recreation site use and preference in the upper Great Lakes region in 1990. The results suggest that fee increases would have negative impacts on at least some of the respondents and reduce choice probability of some sites. The models also suggest that some segments of the population may be more affected by a fee increase than others, but the differences were not easy to explain in terms of socio-demographic characteristics of the segments. Some groups also showed an increase in choice probability at the highest fee levels.

B. Fees as a Tool to Allocate/Ration Use

Many of these papers discuss the potential benefits of using fees to ration use. The authors suggest that, if done appropriately, rationing by price can maximize economic and social benefits by raising revenues, managing congestion, and changing use distribution by rationing demand. These papers also discuss equity concerns such as who should pay, and the potential for fees to exclude users.

Chase, Lisa C.; Lee, David R.; Schulze, William D.; Anderson, Deborah J. 1998. Ecotourism demand and differential pricing of National Park access in Costa Rica. Land Economics. 74(4): 466–482.

Annotation: Little experience exists in developing countries to guide natural resource managers in designing effective pricing strategies for protected areas. After reviewing the current status of ecotourism in Costa Rica, this paper presents a theoretical framework using contingent behavior methodology to assess the effects of differential entrance fees on visitation demand in three Costa Rican National Parks. Primary data were collected from 311 in-person interviews conducted from January to March 1995. Data collected includes information on foreign tourists' hypothetical park visitation behaviors at alternative entrance fee levels. Results show that visitation demand elasticities at the three parks are quite different, and that substitutability in visitation demand can exist between parks with similar attractions. This suggests that differential fees can be an effective tool for distributing tourism use.

Cordell, H. Ken. 1981. Pricing for allocating low-density recreational use between private and commercial users of natural areas. In: Buist, Leon J., ed. Proceedings of the national conference on allocation of recreation opportunities on public land between outfitted and nonoutfitted publics. Publ. R-149. Reno: Nevada Agricultural Experiment Station, College of Agriculture, University of Nevada: 77–103.

Annotation: This paper addresses the recreation use allocation of low-density public recreation resources (rivers, wilderness and wilderness-type areas, and other public lands) between private users and users of commercial outfitting services. The description and analysis of this issue includes the activities of river running, backpacking, and fishing. After reviewing the economics literature and discussing the problem of allocation and rationing, a pricing strategy is introduced. A discriminatory pricing system where different prices are charged at different areas for different activities and for peak and off-peak periods is proposed. This system is an efficient way of distributing use according to consumer demand and producing revenues that are sufficient to cover marginal supply costs. Private and commercial users should be charged the same price.

Fractor, David T. 1982. Evaluating alternative methods for rationing wilderness use. Journal of Leisure Research. 14(4): 341–349.

Annotation: This paper evaluates and compares alternative methods for rationing wilderness use. The analysis assumes a fixed supply of wilderness with free access and excess demand. The rationing methods considered are price, random selection (lottery), queuing (waiting in line), and reservation. Using standard measurements of social benefit (the benefit, in dollars, that accrues to society as a result of voluntary provision of wilderness access), rationing by price maximizes social benefit. Rationing by price guarantees that those who most avidly desire wilderness access (as measured by willingness to pay) will obtain it, and to some degree, wilderness users will also be providing revenue that can be used to expand the wilderness supply.

Manning, Robert E.; Callinan, Elaine A.; Echelberger, Herbert E.; Koenemann, Edward J.; McEwen, Douglas N. 1984. Differential fees: raising revenue, distributing demand. Journal of Parks and Recreation Administration. 2(1): 20–38.

Annotation: See section VII.A. page 22.

McLean, Donald J.; Johnson, Ronald C. A. 1997. Techniques for rationing public recreation services. Journal of Park and Recreation Administration. 15(3): 76–92.

Annotation: Rationing use of public services is proposed as an approach that should be used in response to reductions in public funding support for recreation services. Depending on the general service mission of the organization (resource protection, social values, or personal enrichment), there are a variety of rationing techniques that could be used. Eight rationing techniques are outlined: (1) price; (2) reservations; (3) lotteries; (4) priority based on need; (5) access to use rules, such as skill level; (6) time allotment; (7) demarketing through decreasing public awareness of the service, introducing ancillary services, and not providing a service; and (8) vouchers.

Peterson, George L. 1992. Using fees to manage congestion at recreation areas. In: Waverly, Glen. Park visitor research for better management. Victoria, Canada: Hepper Marriott and Associates: 58–67.

Annotation: The purpose of this paper is review some of the concerns about using fees to manage congestion at recreation areas. Two required conditions for efficient free market price rationing are first discussed. Then the concepts of fixed cost, marginal cost, and transaction cost of collecting fees are reviewed, followed by a discussion of the components of potentially capturable value. Alternative justifications for fees are then examined, with discussion centering on revenue, value capture, demonstration of value for equal treatment in policy decisions, management of demand through price rationing, and social equity policy aimed at redistribution of income.

Next, the question of who should pay is discussed. And finally, the paper turns to a review of various types of fees that can be used for price rationing, legal and political questions that surround price rationing, and the distributional effects of price rationing.

VIII. ESTIMATING AND SPENDING FEE REVENUE

It is important to strike a balance between setting a price to obtain necessary revenue and pricing users out of the market. These papers suggest that visitor attitudes toward fees should be considered when calculating revenue projections from fees. In a study to determine how to spend fee revenues, wilderness respondents favored a spending program to maintain existing conditions rather than improve them. This may indicate that wilderness users expect a different type of product or experience than other recreation users.

Reiling, Stephen D.; Cheng, Hsiang-tai. 1995. Potential revenues from a new day-use fee. In: Proceedings of the 1994 Northeastern recreation research symposium. Gen. Tech. Rep. NE-198. Radnor, PA: U.S. Department of Agriculture, Forest Service, Northeastern Forest Experiment Station: 57–60.

Annotation: In 1984, the Army Corps of Engineers was granted authority to charge fees at its day-use facilities. This paper presents the procedures used to estimate day-use fee revenues and compare the estimated revenue projections to a "naïve" estimate of revenue (which assumes that visitation to the sites would not change after fee implementation). Six fee projects were selected to participate in this study. The questionnaire contained general questions such as the recreational activities of respondents and the types of facilities and services they considered important, and questions about attitude toward fees and the number of trips they would make to the day-use area at alternative fee levels. Over 1,400 surveys were filled out by day users. Almost half of respondents (48.5 percent) agreed they should not have to pay a fee to use the day-use areas, and 40 percent indicated they would not visit the Corps day-use areas if a fee were charged. The projected revenues range from a low of about $900,000 to a high of $1.6 million. Naive projections range from a low of $1.3 million to a high of almost $7 million.

Teasley, R. Jeff; Bergstrom, John C.; Cordell, H. Ken. 1994. Estimating revenue-capture potential associated with public area recreation. Journal of Agricultural and Resource Economics. 19(1): 89–101.

Annotation: This article compares two techniques for measuring the revenue-capture potential from fees. The general study area consisted of two National Forests in the Southeast.

Dichotomous choice contingent valuation (a consumer is given a fixed quantity of a commodity and asked to value the commodity) and trip response (a consumer is given a fixed price and asked to state the quantity he or she would "purchase" at that price) data were collected in onsite interviews with recreationists who were leaving the area. The two revenue-capture strategies produced differing levels of revenue potential. Higher fees will price higher percentages of trips by current users out of the market, thereby reducing revenue potential. Expected visitation appears sensitive to the type of fee payment scheme used. It is possible that the trip response method may provide a more neutral means of asking revenue-capture questions in a survey format.

Vogt, Christine A.; Williams, Daniel R. 1999. Support for wilderness recreation fees: the influence of fee purpose and day versus overnight use. Journal of Park and Recreation Administration. 17(3): 85–99.

Annotation: To evaluate the effect of new fees on public support for spending revenues at the Desolation Wilderness, this paper compares ratings of support for the use of fees for 19 management activities. Support was measured assuming two rationales across two user group samples. One rationale asks about support for fees to improve upon the current level of service, while the other asks about support for fees to provide the current level of service. Data are from a study that surveyed campers and day users at the Desolation Wilderness from 1997 to 1998. The results suggest a spending program to restore and maintain wilderness conditions is favored over a development and new services spending program. Campers were particularly more supportive of maintaining current conditions. Day users were less definitive in their support for maintaining or improving conditions. There was general support for wilderness use fees with strongest support for restoration of human-damaged sites, litter removal, and provision of information on ways to reduce impacts.

IX. RECREATION FEE DEMONSTRATION PROGRAM WEB SITES

These Web sites provide information about the U.S. Federal Recreation Fee Demonstration Program. Under this program, Congress authorized the National Park Service (NPS), U.S. Fish and Wildlife Service (FWS), Bureau of Land Management (BLM), and USDA Forest Service (USFS) to implement and test new fees at a variety of recreation sites. The program allows the participating agencies to retain at least 80 percent of the revenues at the sites where they were collected. Revenue generated from user fees is spent on operation and maintenance of the recreation sites, habitat enhancement, backlogged repair projects, and other projects that provide on-the-ground improvements.

Forest Service Recreational Fee Demonstration Program: Investing in the Great Outdoors, [Online]. Available: http//www.fs.fed.us/recreation/fee_demo/fee_intro.shtml [2001, June 25].

Annotation: This site provides a wide range of Fee Demonstration Program information representing the USFS's perspective. Reports, forest specific information, frequently asked questions, and a forum to comment on the program are all included.

The National Park Service Recreational Fee Demonstration Program, [Online]. Available: http://www.nps.gov/feedemo [2001, June 25].

Annotation: This Web site provides information regarding the Fee Demonstration Program from the perspective of the NPS and includes an overview, fact sheet, current entrance fees, examples of the fee program, reactions from the public and managers, and links to other sites.

Virtual Reading Room at the Office of Policy Analysis (Department of the Interior), [Online]. Available: http//www.doi.gov/nrl/Recfees [2001, June 25].

Annotation: This site provides access to Reports to Congress by the NPS, USFS, FWS, and BLM, as well as other Federal documents regarding the Recreation Fee Demonstration Program.

Wild Wilderness, [Online]. Available: http//www.wildwilderness.org [2001, June 25].

Annotation: Wild Wilderness is a nonprofit, citizen group dedicated to preserving undeveloped recreational opportunities on public lands. Their Web site provides arguments as to why they and others oppose recreational user fees. They believe the American public-at-large should financially support Federal lands.

AUTHOR INDEX

Multiple page number listings result from works cited in more than one section of the document. For articles that appear more than once, an * marks the page containing the annotation.

Rocky Mountain Research Station
240 West Prospect Road
Fort Collins, CO 80526

RMRS
ROCKY MOUNTAIN RESEARCH STATION

The Rocky Mountain Research Station develops scientific information and technology to improve management, protection, and use of the forests and rangelands. Research is designed to meet the needs of National Forest managers, Federal and State agencies, public and private organizations, academic institutions, industry, and individuals.

Studies accelerate solutions to problems involving ecosystems, range, forests, water, recreation, fire, resource inventory, land reclamation, community sustainability, forest engineering technology, multiple use economics, wildlife and fish habitat, and forest insects and diseases. Studies are conducted cooperatively, and applications may be found worldwide.

Research Locations

Flagstaff, Arizona	Reno, Nevada
Fort Collins, Colorado*	Albuquerque, New Mexico
Boise, Idaho	Rapid City, South Dakota
Moscow, Idaho	Logan, Utah
Bozeman, Montana	Ogden, Utah
Missoula, Montana	Provo, Utah
Lincoln, Nebraska	Laramie, Wyoming

*Station Headquarters, Natural Resources Research Center, 2150 Centre Avenue, Building A, Fort Collins, CO 80526

www.ingramcontent.com/pod-product-compliance
Lightning Source LLC
Chambersburg PA
CBHW082201290526
45794CB00008B/3380